*POETS AND
PROPHETS*

# Robert Browning

# BROWNING'S POEMS AND PLAYS

*in order of publication*

*1833*
Pauline

*1835*
Paracelsus

*1837*
Strafford

*1840*
Sordello

*1841*
Bells and Pomegranates I:
Pippa Passes

*1842*
Bells and Pomegranates II:
King Victor and King Charles

*1842 (Nov)*
Bells and Pomegranates III:
Dramatic Lyrics

*1843 (Jan)*
Bells and Pomegranates IV:
The Return of the Druses

*1843 (Feb)*
Bells and Pomegranates V:
A Blot in the Scutcheon

*1844*
Bells and Pomegranates VI:
Colombe's Birthday

*1845*
Bells and Pomegranates VII:
Dramatic Romances and Lyrics

*1846*
Bells and Pomegranates VIII:
Luria; *and* A Soul's Tragedy

*1849*
Poems *(2 vols)*

*1850*
Christmas Eve and Easter Day

*1855*
Men and Women

*1863*
The Poetical Works *(3 vols)*

*1864*
Dramatis Personae

*1868*
The Poetical Works *(6 vols)*

*1868/9*
The Ring and The Book

*1871 (Aug)*
Balaustion's Adventure

*1871 (Dec)*
Prince Hohenstiel-Schwangau

*1872*
Fifine at the Fair

*1873*
Red Cotton Night-Cap
Country

*1875 (April)*
Aristophanes' Apology

*1878 (Nov)*
The Inn Album

*1876*
Pacchiarotto and how he
worked in Distemper

*1877*
The Agamemnon of
Aeschylus

*1878*
La Saisiaz:
The Two Poets of Croisic

*1879*
Dramatic Idyls

*1880*
Dramatic Idyls:
Second Series

*1883*
Jocoseria

*1884*
Ferishtah's Fancies

*1887*
Parleyings with Certain People
of Importance in their Day

*1888/9*
The Poetical Works *(16 vols)*

*1889*
Asolando

# POETS AND PROPHETS

*A selection of poems by*

# Robert Browning

exploring his pilgrimage

of faith

CHOSEN AND
INTRODUCED BY
RUTH
ETCHELLS

A LION BOOK
Tring • Batavia • Sydney

Selection and introductory text copyright © 1988 Ruth Etchells

Published by
**Lion Publishing plc**
Icknield Way, Tring, Herts, England
ISBN 0 7459 1283 4
**Lion Publishing Corporation**
1705 Hubbard Avenue, Batavia, Illinois 60510, USA
ISBN 0 7459 1283 4
**Albatross Books Pty Ltd**
PO Box 320, Sutherland, NSW 2232, Australia
ISBN 0 86760 924 9

First edition 1988

The recommended edition, from which the extracts
in this book are taken is *Robert Browning: The Poems*,
volumes 1 and 2, Pettigrew, Penguin English Poetry, 1981

**British Library Cataloguing in Publication Data**

Browning, Robert, *1812-1889*
  A selection of poems by Robert Browning,
  exploring his faith.—(Poets and
  prophets).
  I. Title   II. Etchells, Ruth   III. Series
  821'.8

ISBN 0-7459-1283-4

Printed in Italy

# CONTENTS

Introduction  6

O·N·E

**The Struggle to Believe**  9

Easter Day  9
Bishop Blougram's Apology  10
A Death in the Desert  12
Christmas-Eve  14

T·W·O

**God of Power, God of Love**  16

Fra Lippo Lippi  17
Pippa Passes  19
Saul  20
Abt Vogler  23
Rabbi ben Ezra  25

T·H·R·E·E

**Eternal Life**  27

Christmas Eve  27
An Epistle... of Karshish  28
Prospice  31

F·O·U·R

**Life in God's Service**  32

Pauline  32
Life in a Love  33
De Gustibus  34
Home-thoughts, from the Sea  36
Epilogue in Asolando  37
Childe Roland to the Dark Tower Came  38
Epilogue from Ferishtah's Fancies  41
Easter Day  43

Notes and Sources  46

# INTRODUCTION

The span of Robert Browning's life (1812-1889) so closely parallels the tumult of the nineteenth century that inevitably his poetry has become identified with it. In our own century, for some decades his reputation suffered with that of the Victorian age in which he lived, dismissed by many as optimistic to the point of smugness. In fact, this was never truly characteristic either of Victorian England or of Browning. Rather, he expresses a strenuous hopefulness achieved in the context of great spiritual, political, social and economic ferment. And it was to this note that his readers eagerly responded. The fact that he spent the whole of his married life (1846-1861) in Italy also means that much of his work grows out of a response to a European, rather than an insular, culture.

Robert Browning was born in Camberwell in May, 1812. His family belonged to the prosperous Victorian merchant classes. Freed from the necessity to earn a living, Browning was therefore able to concentrate all his considerable energy on his artistic and intellectual interests. His father collected a library of several thousand volumes, which formed the most important part of Browning's education. His mother's strongly Protestant piety, with its emphasis on simplicity and orthodoxy, was a stern antidote to the youthful Browning's passionate poetic idealism.

In 1846, after eighteen months' courtship of the invalid poetess, Elizabeth Moulton Barrett, Browning persuaded her not only to leave her sickroom but to marry him secretly and go to live with him in Italy. Fifteen years of happy marriage followed, during the first ten of which Browning's best work was written. Religion was important to Robert Browning and Elizabeth, but religion as it stood at the conjunction of art, history, science, philosophy, morality and belief. It is this many-sided encounter which shapes his poetry and gives it energy.

In recent years a number of critics have presented

Browning's work, and particularly the Christian belief which finds expression in it, much more sympathetically, discovering in it many of the same issues with which believers and agnostics alike contend today. The pressures put upon traditional Christian belief in the nineteenth century by biblical and scientific scholarship and by the new science and industry are well known. The exciting consequence for us is that we find Browning writing from the very heart of issues we ourselves are currently debating, both within and beyond the Christian church. They concern both what is involved in the *nature* of Christian belief, and what is involved in the act of believing—in the face of problems posed by the intellectual climate of the day and by the divisions and aberrations of the church itself. In wrestling honestly with these questions, Browning gave expression to a hard-won faith which did not substantially change through most of his writing, though its emphases altered, as did the poetic methods by which he explored it. He began in *Pauline* from an exceedingly personal exposition which betrayed the clamant needs of the self, the 'soul', as the starting-point of his religious quest. Society—and the critics—were unimpressed. Sales were rock-bottom. And he moved from this style to a different medium: exploring issues more objectively by dramatizing them through a character or a situation.

At the heart of Browning's religious struggle was his passionate sense of the transcendence of God—the unknowable Divine. Yet, paradoxically, the Christian faith affirmed a God who made himself known through the incarnation. God in Christ took on our human nature. Running with Browning's sense of God as transcendent was his emphasis on the *power* of God: running with his recognition of the God as very near to us in the incarnation was his sense of the *love* of God. His most effective poetry brings together these two aspects of God's nature and his relationship with humankind.

In this brief selection from his verse we follow Browning as he explores how these three things, human religious aspiration, God's power and God's love are woven together in the Christian faith and in the life of humanity. He rightly takes one of the central beliefs of the Christian faith—the resurrection of Christ and the promise of immortality—as revealing the mystery of a God in whom power and love conjoin. Hence much of his most moving verse. But these high beliefs are firmly rooted in his shrewd and imaginative perception of the loves, hates, longings and fears of human beings, and it is through these that he presents his own doubts and his own beliefs. There is always a questioning, even in his strongest affirmation, and always an affirmation, even in his most perplexed doubting.

The length of most of Browning's poems, let alone their tortuousness, has inevitably meant that much of this selection is made up of extracts. Dots or a line space indicate where material has been omitted between extracts from the same poem. The 'Notes and Sources' at the end of the book give details, including the line numbers, of the material used. Inevitably, any selection must omit much that could (and to some minds ought to) have been included, and to that extent it is a personal choice. If, however, what is in this volume leads readers to explore the fulness of the poems as Browning wrote them, and so to engage with a mind and spirit of arduous and venturesome faith, then it will have succeeded in its—limited—intention. The poet himself always saw the Good beyond the good achieved: and so heaven, most of all.

## O·N·E
# The Struggle to Believe

... The sum of all is—yes, my doubt is great,
My faith's still greater, then my faith's enough.
Bishop Blougram's Apology

In the first is the last, in thy will is my
power to believe.     Saul

Through all Browning's poetry runs his struggle with Christian belief. How to think honestly, face the issues raised by his age, and yet overcome doubt? How and in what sense to rely on the Bible, in the light of new scholarship? How to find Christ amidst the (often arrogant and vainglorious) claims of competing churches and their forms of worship? Browning's world set in motion questions we struggle with still, perhaps even more intensely.

### F·R·O·M
## Easter Day

How very hard it is to be
A Christian! Hard for you and me...
To realize it, more or less,
With even the moderate success
Which commonly repays our strife
To carry out the aims of life...

...At first you say, 'The whole or chief
Of difficulties, is belief.'
Could I believe once thoroughly,
The rest were simple...
Prove to me, only that the least
Command of God is God's indeed,
And what injunction shall I need
To pay obedience?

## Bishop Blougram's Apology

Unbelief creates as many intellectual and moral problems as belief. Yet if God is, and is good, then he must long since have acted. If so, when, where and how?

*Bishop Blougram, a worldly and sophisticated prelate, is defending his own ambiguous belief:*

Why first, you don't believe, you don't and can't,
(Not statedly, that is, and fixedly
And absolutely and exclusively)
In any revelation called divine.
No dogmas nail your faith; and what remains
But say so, like the honest man you are?
First, therefore, overhaul theology!
Nay, I too, not a fool, you please to think,
Must find believing every whit as hard:
And if I do not frankly say as much,
The ugly consequence is clear enough.

Now wait, my friend: well, I do not believe—
If you'll accept no faith that is not fixed,
Absolute and exclusive, as you say.
You're wrong—I mean to prove it in due time.
Meanwhile, I know where difficulties lie
I could not, cannot solve, nor ever shall,
So give up hope accordingly to solve—
(To you, and over the wine). Our dogmas then
With both of us, though in unlike degree,
Missing full credence—overboard with them!
I mean to meet you on your own premise:
Good, there go mine in company with yours!

And now what are we? unbelievers both,
Calm and complete, determinately fixed
Today, to-morrow and for ever, pray?
You'll guarantee me that? Not so, I think!
In no wise! all we've gained is, that belief,

As unbelief before, shakes us by fits,
Confounds us like its predecessor. Where's
The gain? how can we guard our unbelief,
Make it bear fruit to us—the problem here.
Just when we are safest, there's a sunset-touch,
A fancy from a flower-bell, someone's death,
A chorus-ending from Euripides,—
And that's enough for fifty hopes and fears
As old and new at once as nature's self,
To rap and knock and enter in our soul,
Take hands and dance there, a fantastic ring,
Round the ancient idol, on his base again,—
The grand Perhaps! We look on helplessly.
There the old misgivings, crooked questions are—
This good God,—what he could do, if he would,
Would, if he could—then must have done long since:
If so, when, where and how? some way must be,—
Once feel about, and soon or late you hit
Some sense, in which it might be, after all.
Why not, 'The Way, the Truth, the Life'?

## F·R·O·M
## A Death in the Desert

Questions about the truth of the Bible were finding acute expression in Browning's lifetime, in the so-called 'Higher Criticism' which explored sources, forms of writing, authorship and date. In response, Browning imagines the apostle John, dying at a great age, hearing current heresies and glimpsing those to come. As he dies, he speaks simply of the calling he has faithfully obeyed: to speak and to write of the facts of Christ as he knew him, in order to help men and women believe.

*The dying apostle is speaking:*

'How will it be when none more saith "I saw"?

'Such ever was love's way: to rise, it stoops.
Since I, whom Christ's mouth taught, was bidden teach
I went, for many years, about the world,
Saying "It was so; so I heard and saw,"
Speaking as the case asked: and men believed.
Afterward came the message to myself
In Patmos isle; I was not bidden teach,
But simply listen, take a book and write,
Nor set down other than the given word.
With nothing left to my arbitrament
To choose or change: I wrote and men believed.

Then, for my time grew brief, no message more,
No call to write again, I found a way,
And, reasoning from my knowledge, merely taught
Men should, for love's sake, in love's strength believe;
Or I would pen a letter to a friend
And urge the same as friend, nor less nor more:
Friends said I reasoned rightly, and believed.
But at the last, why, I seemed left alive
Like a sea-jelly weak on Patmos strand,
To tell dry sea-beach gazers how I fared
When there was mid-sea, and the mighty things;
Left to repeat, "I saw I heard I knew."...
'...Men said, "It is getting long ago:
Where is the promise of His coming?"—asked
These young ones in their strength, and loth to wait
Of me who, when their sires were born, was old.
I, for I loved them, answered, joyfully,
Since I was there, and helpful in my age;
And, in the main, I think such men believed...
...Yet now I wake in such decrepitude
As I had slidden down and fallen afar,
Past even the presence of my former self,
Grasping the while for stay at facts which snap,
Till I am found arising from my own world,
Feeling for foothold through a blank profound,
Along with unborn people in strange lands,
Who say—I hear said or conceive they say—
"Was John at all, and did he say he saw?
Assure us, ere we ask what he might see!"

And how shall I assure them?...

'...Just thus, ye needs must apprehend what truth
I see, reduced to plain historic fact,
Diminished into clearness, proved a point
And far away:

'I say, the acknowledgement of God in Christ
Accepted by thy reason, solves for thee,
All questions in the earth and out of it.'

## FROM
## CHRISTMAS–EVE

Like his wife Elizabeth, Browning had a 'dissenting' (that is, nonconformist) background, and their letters, such as the one below, reflect the difficulty both felt in finding real satisfaction in any of the competing patterns of worship offered by 'rival' churches. Hardest of all to bear was the claim pressed by each denomination that its way was the only right and proper way, not only to worship, but to know, God. Both liked 'beyond comparison best the simplicity of the dissenters', while finding 'enough to dissent from' even amongst them. The largeness of Browning's spirit, however, led him, in advance of his times, to recognize how each style of worship complemented the others and how together they could lead us to God:

> Look at that injunction to 'love God with all the heart and soul and strength'—and then imagine yourself bidding any faculty, that arises towards the love of him, be still! If in a meeting house, with the blank white walls and a simple doctrinal exposition,—all the senses should turn (from where they be neglected) to all that sunshine in the Sistine with its music and painting, which would lift them at once to Heaven—why should you not go forth—to return just as quickly, when they are nourished into a luxuriousness that extinguishes what is called, Reason's pale wavering light, lamp or whatever it is…There seems no longer need of earnestness in assertion, or proof… so it runs lightly over, like foam on the top of a wave.

The poem 'Christmas Eve' * grows from this struggle. In it the central figure finds himself, one Christmas Eve, not easily belonging to any of the different churches. But his struggle with their competing claims leads him to a fresh affirmation of his personal relationship with Christ: 'I only know he named my name.'

* See note on page 47.

After how many modes, this Christmas-Eve,
Does the self-same weary thing take place?
The same endeavour to make you believe,
And with much the same effect, no more:
Each method abundantly convincing,
As I say, to those convinced before,
But scarce to be swallowed without wincing
By the not-as-yet-convinced. For me,
I have my own church equally:
And in this church my faith sprang first!...
Needs must there be one way, our chief
Best way of worship: let me strive
To find it, and when found, contrive
My fellows also take their share!
This constitutes my earthly care:
God's is above it and distinct.
For I, a man, with men am linked
And not a brute with brutes; no gain
That I experience, must remain
Unshared: but should my best endeavour
To share it, fail—subsisteth ever
God's care above, and I exult
That God, by God's own ways occult,
May—doth, I will believe—bring back
All wanderers to a single track.
Meantime, I can but testify
God's care for me—no more, can I—
It is but for myself I know;
Have I been sure, this Christmas-Eve,
God's own hand did the rainbow weave,
Whereby the truth from heaven slid
Into my soul?—I cannot bid
The world admit he stooped to heal
My soul, as if in a thunder-peal
Where one heard noise, and one saw flame,
I only knew he named my name.

## T·W·O
# GOD OF POWER, GOD OF LOVE

> ... to comprehend the works of God
> And God himself, and all God's intercourse
> With human mind.
> PARACELSUS

> 'Is not God now i' the world His power first made?
> Is not His love at issue still with sin
> Visibly when a wrong is done on earth?'
> A DEATH IN THE DESERT

Browning's belief in the God shown by Jesus Christ remained strenuously struggling, yet in most basics unchanged, through most of his work. Browning was naturally attracted by the great oppositions of 'power' and 'love'. And it was the unique Christian message of the transcendent Divine Power which was *also* absolute Divine Love which inspired some of his most moving verse. God as Love seized his heart.

The inequities of human life, and how God may be perceived as 'just' within them, preoccupy much of his writing. God is 'just' only from a perspective beyond time: yet the vision of that justness is present here to the eye of faith. In several dramatic monologues, extracts from two of which appear here, Browning explores this. This section begins, however, with Browning's vision of God as Creator of the good world and all that is in it, and of how humankind may respond to its beauty. The song from 'Pippa Passes' (included here), which is so often quoted as an example of Browning's facile optimism, is in fact put in the mouth of a badly treated factory girl, whose delight in God's world preserves her from bitterness and this shows up the cheapness and lack of depth of other more materialistic forms of pleasure.

F·R·O·M
## Fra Lippo Lippi

I n this dramatic monologue the artist-monk, Fra Lippo Lippi, caught outside the monastery walls after curfew by the city watch, speaks of his conviction that all the sensuous delights of the world are given by a good God. It is the task of the artist to work with the Creator to help his fellows see, as they have never seen before, the beauty and wonder—and pain and mystery—of the world, and humankind in it: and so doing, to glorify God and hate evil.

*The artist-monk is speaking:*

If you get simple beauty and naught else,
You get about the best thing God invents:
That's somewhat: and you'll find the soul you have missed,
Within yourself, when you return him thanks.
For me, I think I speak as I was taught;
I always see the garden and God there
A-making man's wife: and, my lesson learned,

The value and significance of flesh,
I can't unlearn ten minutes afterwards...
     You be judge!
You speak no Latin more than I, belike;
However, you're my man, you've seen the world
—The beauty and the wonder and the power,
The shapes of things, their colours, lights and shades,
Changes, surprises,—and God made it all!
—For what? Do you feel thankful, ay or no,
For this fair town's face, yonder river's line,
The mountain round it and the sky above,
Much more the figures of man, woman, child,
These are the frame to? What's it all about?
To be passed over, despised? or dwelt upon,
Wondered at? oh, this last of course!—you say.
But why not do as well as say,—paint these
Just as they are, careless what comes of it?
God's works—paint anyone, and count it crime
To let a truth slip. Don't object, 'His works
Are here already; nature is complete:
Suppose you reproduce her'—(which you can't)
'There's no advantage! you must beat her, then.'
For, don't you mark? we're made so that we love
First when we see them painted, things we have passed
Perhaps a hundred times nor cared to see;
And so they are better, painted—better to us,
Which is the same thing. Art was given for that;
God uses us to help each other so,
Lending our minds out. Have you noticed, now,
Your cullion's hanging face? A bit of chalk,
And trust me but you should, though! How much more,
If I drew higher things with the same truth!
That were to take the Prior's pulpit-place,
Interpret God to all of you! Oh, oh,
It makes me mad to see what men shall do
And we in our graves! This world's no blot for us,
Nor blank; it means intensely, and means good:
To find its meaning is my meat and drink.

F·R·O·M
## Pippa Passes

This long poem is chiefly remembered now for the songs sung by Pippa, whose innocent joy pierces the hearts of those who hear her, and changes their understanding of how they should judge the different situations in which they find themselves.

*The year's at the spring
And day's at the morn;
Morning's at seven;
The hill-side's dew-pearled;
The lark's on the wing;
The snail's on the thorn:
God's in his heaven—
All's right with the world!*

[PIPPA *passes*]
SEBALD: God's in his heaven! Do you hear that?
Who spoke?...

OTTIMA: Oh—that little ragged girl!
She must have rested on the step: we give them
But this one holiday the whole year round.
Did you ever see our silk-mills—their inside?
There are ten silk-mills now belong to you.
She stoops to pick my double heartsease...

# FROM
## SAUL

In this, perhaps the best known of all Browning's dramatic monologues, David has been sent for to soothe with his music the suffering King Saul. Only partly able to dispel the black depression which is destroying his king, the young harpist is so moved by love and longing to effect healing, that he bursts through into a vision of God's love for the world.

*David is speaking at the height of his vision:*

'I have gone the whole round of creation:
  I saw and I spoke:
I, a work of God's hand for that purpose,
  received in my brain
And pronounced on the rest of his handwork—
  returned him again
His creation's approval or censure: I spoke as I saw:
I report as a man may of God's work—all's love,
  yet all's law.
Now I lay down the judgeship he lent me. Each faculty tasked
To perceive him, has gained an abyss, where a dew-drop was asked
Have I knowledge? confounded it shrivels at Wisdom laid bare.
Have I forethought? how purblind, how blank, to the Infinite Care.
Do I task any faculty highest, to image success?
I but open my eyes,—and perfection, no more and no less
In the kind I imagined, full-fronts me, and God is seen God
In the star, in the stone, in the flesh, in the soul and the clod.
And thus looking within and around me, I ever renew
(With that stoop of the soul which in bending upraises it too)
The submission of man's nothing-perfect to God's all-complete,
As by each new obeisance in spirit, I climb to his feet,
Yet with all this abounding experience, this deity known,
I shall dare to discover some province, some gift of my own
There's a faculty pleasant to exercise, hard to hood-wink,

I am fain to keep still in abeyance, (I laugh as I think)
Lest, insisting to claim and parade in it, wot ye, I worst
E'en the Giver in one gift.—Behold, I could love if I durst!
But I sink the pretension as fearing a man may o'ertake
God's own speed in the one way of love: I abstain for
   love's sake.
—What, my soul? see thus far and no farther? when doors
   great and small,
Nine-and-ninety flew ope at our touch, should the
   hundredth appal?
In the least things have faith, yet distrust in the greatest
   of all?
Do I find love so full in my nature, God's ultimate gift,
That I doubt his own love can compete with it? Here,
   the parts shift?
Here, the creature surpass the Creator,—the end, what
   Began?
Would I fain in my impotent yearning do all for this man,
And dare doubt he alone shall not help him, who yet alone can?
Would it ever have entered my mind, the bare will, much
   less power,
To bestow on this Saul what I sang of, the marvellous
   dower
Of the life he was gifted and filled with? to make such
   a soul,
Such a body, and then such an earth for insphering the
   whole?
And doth it not enter my mind (as my warm tears attest)
These good things being given, to go on, and give one
   more, the best?
Ay, to save and redeem and restore him, maintain at the
   height
This perfection,—succeed with life's dayspring, death's
   minute of night?
Interpose at the difficult minute, snatch Saul the mistake,
Saul the failure, the ruin he seems now,—and bid him
   awake
From the dream, the probation, the prelude, to find
   himself set
Clear and safe in new light and new life,—a new harmony yet
To be run, and continued, and ended—who knows?—
   or endure!
The man taught enough, by life's dream, of the rest to
   make sure;
By the pain-throb, triumphantly winning intensified bliss,

And the next world's reward and repose, by the struggles in this.

'I believe it!' 'Tis thou, God, that givest, 'tis I who receive:
In the first is the last, in thy will is my power to believe.
All's one gift: thou canst grant it moreover, as prompt to my prayer
As I breathe out this breath, as I open these arms to the air.
From thy will, stream the worlds, life and nature, thy dread Sabaoth:
*I* will?—the mere atoms despise me! Why am I not loth
To look that, even that in the face too? Why is it I dare
Think but lightly of such impuissance? What stops my despair?
This;—'tis not what man Does which exalts him, but what man would do!
See the King—I would help him but cannot, the wishes fall through.
Could I wrestle to raise him from sorrow, grow poor to enrich,
To fill up his life, starve my own out, I would—knowing which,
I know that my service is perfect. Oh, speak through me now!
Would I suffer for him that I love? So wouldst thou—so wilt thou!
So shall crown thee the topmost, ineffablest, uttermost crown—
And thy love fill infinitude wholly, nor leave up nor down
One spot for the creature to stand in! It is by no breath,
Turn of eye, wave of hand, that salvation joins issue with death!
As thy Love is discovered almighty, almighty be proved
Thy power, that exists with and for it, of being Beloved!
He who did most, shall bear most; the strongest shall stand the most weak.
'Tis the weakness in strength, that I cry for! my flesh, that I seek
In the Godhead! I seek and I find it. O Saul, it shall be
A Face like my face that receives thee; a Man like to me,
Thou shalt love and be loved by, for ever: a Hand like this hand
Shall throw open the gates of new life to thee! See the Christ stand!

I n the two extracts that follow, the two speakers,—the first a musician and the second a famous rabbi—muse on how the circumstances of life contrast, with our sense of what ought to be; so that we are filled with a sense of the waste and injustice of life. Against this, Abt Vogler in the first extract, and Rabbi ben Ezra in the second, affirm their conviction that the Eternal God, who gave us our sense of good and of justice will, in the perspective of eternity, fulfil these desires. No good that we have loved will ever be lost, and the completion of our life will prove its—and our— value to God.

F·R·O·M
## Abt Vogler

*The musician is speaking:*

Therefore to whom turn I but to thee, the ineffable Name?
  Builder and maker, thou, of houses not made with hands!
What, have fear of change from thee who art ever the same?
  Doubt that thy power can fill the heart that thy power expands?
There shall never be one lost good! What was, shall live as before
The evil is null, is naught, is silence implying sound;
What was good shall be good, with, for evil, so much good more;
  On the earth the broken arcs; in the heaven, a perfect round.

All we have willed or hoped or dreamed of good shall
  exist;
  Not its semblance, but itself; no beauty, nor good, nor
    power
Whose voice has gone forth, but each survives for the
  melodist
  When eternity affirms the conception of an hour.
The high that proved too high, the heroic for earth too
  hard,
  The passion that left the ground to lose itself in the sky,
Are music sent up to God by the lover and the bard;
  Enough that he heard it once: we shall hear it by-and-by.

And what is our failure here but a triumph's evidence
  For the fulness of the days? Have we withered or
    agonized?
Why else was the pause prolonged but that singing might
  issue thence?
  Why rushed the discords in but that harmony should
    be prized?
Sorrow is hard to bear, and doubt is slow to clear,
  Each sufferer says his say, his scheme of the weal and
    woe:
But God has a few of us whom he whispers in the ear;
  The rest may reason and welcome: 'tis we musicians
    know.

F·R·O·M
## Rabbi Ben Ezra

*The rabbi is speaking:*

Grow old along with me!
The best is yet to be,
The last of life, for which the first was made:
   Our times are in His hand
   Who saith 'A whole I planned,
Youth shows but half; trust God: see all nor be afraid!'...

Youth ended, I shall try
My gain or loss thereby;
Leave the fire ashes, what survives is gold:
   And I shall weigh the same,
   Give life its praise or blame:
Young, all lay in dispute; I shall know, being old.

For note, when evening shuts,
A certain moment cuts
The deed off, calls the glory from the grey:
   A whisper from the west
   Shoots—'Add this to the rest,
Take it and try its worth: here dies another day.'

So, still within this life,
Though lifted o'er its strife,
Let me discern, compare, pronounce at last,
   'This rage was right i' the main,
   That acquiescence vain:
The Future I may face now I have proved the Past.'

For more is not reserved
To man, with soul just nerved
To act tomorrow what he learns today:
   Here, work enough to watch
   The Master work, and catch
Hints of the proper craft, tricks of the tool's true play...

Thoughts hardly to be packed
Into a narrow act,

Fancies that broke through language and escaped;
  All I could never be,
  All, men ignored in me,
This, I was worth to God, whose wheel the pitcher shaped.

  Ay, note that Potter's wheel,
  That metaphor! and feel
Why time spins fast, why passive lies our clay,—
  Thou, to whom fools propound,
  When the wine makes its round,
'Since life fleets, all is change; the Past gone, seize today!'

  Fool! All that is, at all,
  Lasts ever, past recall;
Earth changes, but thy soul and God stand sure:
  What entered into thee,
  *That* was, is, and shall be:
Time's wheel runs back or stops: Potter and clay endure...

  But I need, now as then,
  Thee, God, who mouldest men;
And since, not even while the whirl was worst,
  Did I,—to the wheel of life
  With shapes and colours rife,
Bound dizzily,—mistake my end, to slake Thy thirst:

  So, take and use Thy work:
  Amend what flaws may lurk,
What strain o' the stuff, what warpings past the aim!
  My times be in Thy hand!
  Perfect the cup as planned!
Let age approve of youth, and death complete the same!

# T·H·R·E·E
# Eternal Life

The hope of the life of heaven, the resurrection life, is one of the strongest themes in Browning's poetry. It was a conviction he shared with his wife, who wrote to him before their marriage of her sense of God beyond the sects and denominations, concluding, 'when the veil of the body falls, how we shall look into each other's faces, astonished—after one glance at God's!'\*

### F·R·O·M
### Christmas Eve

> Earth breaks up, time drops away,
> In flows heaven, with its new day
> Of endless life, when He who trod
> Very man and very God,
> This earth in weakness, shame and pain,
> Dying the death whose signs remain
> Up yonder on the accursed tree,
> Shall come again, no more to be
> Of captivity the thrall,
> But the one God, All in All,
> King of Kings, Lord of Lords,
> As His servant John received the words,
> 'I died, and live for evermore!'

---

\* See note on 'Christmas Eve', page 47.

## FROM
## AN EPISTLE...OF KARSHISH

Typically, Browning explored the mysteries of the resurrection through the character of a physician who encounters Lazarus many years after Christ raised him from the dead. The disturbing questions which run through his mind are recounted in a letter to a fellow physician. In this excerpt he begins to tell the story:

> And first—the man's own firm conviction rests
> That he was dead (in fact they buried him)
> —That he was dead and then restored to life
> By a Nazarene physician of his tribe:
> —'Sayeth, the same bade 'Rise,' and he did rise.
> 'Such cases are diurnal,' thou wilt cry.
> Not so this figment!—not, that such a fume,
> Instead of giving way to time and health,
> Should eat itself into the life of life,
> As saffron tingeth flesh, blood, bones and all!
> For see, how he takes up the after-life.
> The man—it is one Lazarus a Jew,
> Sanguine, proportioned, fifty years of age,
> The body's habit wholly laudable,
> As much, indeed, beyond the common health
> As he were made and put aside to show...
> He holds on firmly to some thread of life—
> (It is the life to lead perforcedly)
> Which runs across some vast distracting orb
> Of glory on either side that meagre thread,
> Which, conscious of, he must not enter yet—
> The spiritual life around the earthly life:
> The law of that is known to him as this,
> His heart and brain move there, his feet stay here.
> So is the man perplext with impulses
> Sudden to start off crosswise, not straight on,
> Proclaiming what is right and wrong across,
> And not along, this black thread through the blaze—
> 'It should be' balked by 'here it cannot be.'
> And oft the man's soul springs into his face

As if he saw again and heard again
His sage that bade him 'Rise' and he did rise.
Something, a word, a tick o' the blood within
Admonishes: then back he sinks at once
To ashes, who was very fire before,
In sedulous recurrence to his trade
Whereby he earneth him the daily bread;
And studiously the humbler for that pride,
Professedly the faultier that he knows
God's secret, while he holds the thread of life.
Indeed the especial marking of the man
Is prone submission to the heavenly will—
Seeing it, what it is, and why it is.
'Sayeth, he will wait patient to the last
For that same death which must restore his being
To equilibrium, body loosening soul
Divorced even now by premature full growth:
He will live, nay, it pleaseth him to live
So long as God please, and just how God please.
He even seeketh not to please God more
(Which meaneth, otherwise) than as God please...

 Thou wilt object—Why have I not ere this
Sought out the sage himself, the Nazarene
Who wrought this cure, inquiring at the source,
Conferring with the frankness that befits?
Alas! it grieveth me, the learned leech
Perished in a tumult many years ago,
Accused,—our learning's fate,—of wizardry,
Rebellion, to the setting up a rule
And creed prodigious as described to me.
His death, which happened when the earthquake fell
(Prefiguring, as soon appeared, the loss
To occult learning in our lord the sage
Who lived there in the pyramid alone)
Was wrought by the mad people—that's their wont!
On vain recourse, as I conjecture it,
To his tried virtue, for miraculous help—
How could he stop the earthquake? That's their way!
The other imputations must be lies:

But take one, though I loathe to give it thee,
In mere respect for any good man's fame.
(And after all, our patient Lazarus
Is stark mad; should we count on what he says?
Perhaps not: though in writing to a leech
'Tis well to keep back nothing of a case.)
This man so cured regards the curer, then,
As—God forgive me! who but God himself,
Creator and sustainer of the world,
That came and dwelt in flesh on it awhile!
—'Sayeth that such an one was born and lived,
Taught, healed the sick, broke bread at his own house,
Then died, with Lazarus by, for aught I know,
And yet was...what I said nor choose repeat,
And must have so avouched himself, in fact,
In hearing of this very Lazarus...

   The very God! think, Abib; dost thou think?
So, the All-Great, were the All-Loving too—
So, through the thunder comes a human voice
Saying, 'O heart I made, a heart beats here!
Face, my hands fashioned, see it in myself!
Thou hast no power nor mayst conceive of mine,
But love I gave thee, with myself to love,
And thou must love me who have died for thee!'
The madman saith He said so: it is strange.

## Prospice

Browning wrote in his wife's *New Testament*, shortly after her death, 'This I believe, this I affirm, this I am certain it is, that from this life I shall pass to another, there, where the lady lives of whom my soul was enamoured.' About the same time, he wrote this poem:

Fear death?—to feel the fog in my throat,
    The mist in my face,
When the snows begin, and the blasts denote
    I am nearing the place,
The power of the night, the press of the storm,
    The post of the foe;
Where he stands, the Arch Fear in a visible form,
    Yet the strong man must go:
For the journey is done and the summit attained,
    And the barriers fall,
Though a battle's to fight ere the guerdon be gained,
    The reward of it all.
I was ever a fighter, so—one fight more,
    The best and the last!
I would hate that death bandaged my eyes, and forbore,
    And bade me creep past.
No! let me taste the whole of it, fare like my peers
    The heroes of old,
Bear the brunt, in a minute pay glad life's arrears
    Of pain, darkness and cold.
For sudden the worst turns the best to the brave,
    The black minute's at end,
And the elements' rage, the fiend-voices that rave,
    Shall dwindle, shall blend,
Shall change, shall become first a peace out of pain,
    Then a light, then thy breast,
O thou soul of my soul! I shall clasp thee again,
    And with God be the rest.

# F·O·U·R
# LIFE IN GOD'S SERVICE

*All service ranks the same with God:*
*If now, as formerly he trod*
*Paradise, his presence fills*

*Our earth, each only as God wills*
*Can work—God's puppets, best and worst,*
*Are we; there is no last nor first.*
PIPPA PASSES

B rowning's response to his belief in, and love of, God, is highly active. It is one of loving, striving, enduring, and answering to God's judgement as eternity is faced. He sees humankind valued by God equally in all its service, great or small.

God's love is central to Browning's faith. It calls out, in response, a love for God, a delight in the love between man and woman (Browning's love lyrics are among the best known of his poems) and a passionate love of place.

### F·R·O·M
### PAULINE

And what is that I hunger for but God?
My God, my God, let me for once look on thee
As though nought else existed, we alone!
And as creation crumbles, my soul's spark
Expands till I can say,—Even from myself
I need thee and I feel thee and I love thee.
I do not plead my rapture in thy works
For love of thee, nor that I feel as one
Who cannot die: but there is that in me
Which turns to thee, which loves or which should love.

## LIFE IN A LOVE

Escape me?
Never—
Beloved!
While I am I, and you are you,
 So long as the world contains us both,
 Me the loving and you the loth,
While the one eludes, must the other pursue.
My life is a fault at last, I fear:
 It seems too much like a fate, indeed!
 Though I do my best I shall scarce succeed.
But what if I fail of my purpose here?
It is but to keep the nerves at strain,
 To dry one's eyes and laugh at a fall,
And, baffled, get up and begin again,—
 So the chase takes up one's life, that's all.
While, look but once from your farthest bound
 At me so deep in the dust and dark,
No sooner the old hope goes to ground
 Than a new one, straight to the self-same mark,
I shape me—
Ever
Removed!

## De Gustibus

Your ghost will walk, you lover of trees,
   (If our loves remain)
   In an English lane,
By a cornfield-side a-flutter with poppies.
Hark, those two in the hazel coppice—
A boy and a girl, if the good fates please,
   Making love, say,—
   The happier they!
Draw yourself up from the light of the moon,
And let them pass, as they will too soon,
   With the bean-flowers' boon,
   And the blackbird's tune,
   And May, and June!

II
What I love best in all the world
Is a castle, precipice-encurled,
In a gash of the wind-grieved Apennine.
Or look for me, old fellow of mine,
(If I get my head from out the mouth
O' the grave, and loose my spirit's bands,
And come again to the land of lands)—
In a sea-side house to the farther South,
Where the baked cicada dies or drouth,
And one sharp tree—'tis a cypress—stands,

By the many hundred years red-rusted,
Rough iron-spiked, ripe fruit-o'ercrusted,
My sentinel to guard the sands
To the water's edge. For, what expands
Before the house, but the great opaque
Blue breadth of sea without a break?
While, in the house, for ever crumbles
Some fragment of the frescoed walls,
From blisters where a scorpion sprawls.
A girl bare-footed brings, and tumbles
Down on the pavement, green-flesh melons,
And says there's news today—the king
Was shot at, touched in the liver-wing,
Goes with his Bourbon arm in a sling.
She hopes they have not caught the felons.
Italy, my Italy!
Queen Mary's saying serves for me—
(When fortune's malice
Lost her—Calais)—
Open my heart and you will see
Graved inside of it, 'Italy'.
Such lovers old are I and she:
So it always was, so shall ever be!

## Home-Thoughts, from the Sea

Nobly, nobly Cape Saint Vincent to the North-west died away;
Sunset ran, one glorious blood-red, reeking into Cadiz Bay;
Bluish' mid the burning water, full in face Trafalgar lay;
In the dimmest North-east distance dawned Gibraltar grand and grey;
'Here and here did England help me: how can I help England?'—say,
Whoso turns as I, this evening, turn to God to praise and pray,
While Jove's planet rises yonder, silent over Africa.

'Ah, but a man's reach should exceed his grasp, Or what's a heaven for?' (ANDREA DEL SARTO) Browning's conviction was that 'striving', however ineffectively, was in itself one of the highest of human virtues. His poetry reflects the driving force of passionate aspiration—reaching outwards and forwards—which characterized him to the end. Close to the end of his life he described himself in these terms:

F·R·O·M
## EPILOGUE IN ASOLANDO

'One who never turned his back but marched breast forward,
Never doubted clouds would break,
Never dreamed, though right were worsted, wrong would triumph,
Held we fall to rise, are baffled to fight better,
Sleep to wake.

No, at noonday in the bustle of man's work-time
Greet the unseen with a cheer!
Gid him forward, breast and back as either should be,
'Strive and thrive!' cry 'Speed,—fight on, fare ever
There as here!'

F·R·O·M
## CHILDE ROLAND TO THE DARK TOWER CAME

This is perhaps the most haunting of Browning's poems, and certainly the most mysterious. It is the ancient and recurrent tale of the hero on a quest doomed to failure, who yet perseveres to the end and, at his last moment, facing his doom, confronts the terror ahead and challenges it undaunted.

*The hero is speaking:*

Thus, I had so long suffered in this quest,
   Heard failure prophesied so oft, been writ
   So many times among 'The Band'—to wit,
The knights who to the Dark Tower's search addressed
Their steps—that just to fail as they, seemed best,
   And all the doubt was now—should I be fit?...

So, on I went. I think I never saw
   Such starved ignoble nature; nothing throve:
   For flowers—as well expect a cedar grove!
But cockle, spurge, according to their law
Might propagate their kind, with none to awe,
   You'd think; a burr had been a treasure-trove...

As for the grass, it grew as scant as hair
   In leprosy; thin dry blades pricked the mud
   Which underneath looked kneaded up with blood.
One stiff blind horse, his every bone a-stare,
Stood stupefied, however he came there:
   Thrust out past service from the devil's stud!...

A sudden little river crossed my path
   As unexpected as a serpent comes.
   No sluggish tide congenial to the glooms;
This, as it frothed by, might have been a bath
For the fiend's glowing hoof—to see the wrath
   Of its black eddy bespate with flakes and spumes.

So petty yet so spiteful! All along,
  Low scrubbly alders kneeled down over it;
  Drenched willows flung them headlong in a fit
Of mute despair, a suicidal throng:
The river which had done them all the wrong,
  Whate'er that was, rolled by, deterred no whit.

Which, while I forded,—good saints, how I feared
  To set my foot upon a dead man's cheek,
  Each step, or feel the spear I thrust to seek
For hollows, tangled in his hair or beard!
—It may have been a water-rat I speared,
  But, ugh! it sounded like a baby's shriek...

And just as far as ever from the end!
  Naught in the distance but the evening, naught
  To point my footstep further! At the thought,
A great black bird, Apollyon's bosom-friend,
Sailed past, nor beat his wide wing dragon-penned
  That brushed my cap—perchance the guide I sought.

For, looking up, aware I somehow grew,
  'Spite of the dusk, the plain had given place
  All round to mountains—with such name to grace
Mere ugly heights and heaps now stolen in view.
How thus they had surprised me,—solve it, you!
  How to get from them was no clearer case.

Yet half I seemed to recognize some trick
  Of mischief happened to me, God knows when—
  In a bad dream perhaps. Here ended, then,
Progress this way. When, in the very nick
Of giving up, one time more, came a click
  As when a trap shuts—you're inside the den!

Burningly it came on me all at once,
  This was the place! those two hills on the right,
  Crouched like two bulls locked horn in horn in fight;
While to the left, a tall scalped mountain...Dunce,
Dotard, a-dozing at the very nonce,
  After a life spent training for the sight!

What in the midst lay but the Tower itself?
    The round squat turret, blind as the fool's heart,
    Built of brown stone, without a counterpart
In the whole world. The tempest's mocking elf
Points to the shipman thus the unseen shelf
    He strikes on, only when the timbers start.

Not see? because of night perhaps?—why, day
    Came back again for that! before it left,
    The dying sunset kindled through a cleft:
The hills, like giants at a hunting, lay,
Chin upon hand, to see the game at bay,—
    'Now stab and end the creature—to the heft!'

Not hear? when noise was everywhere! it tolled
    Increasing like a bell. Names in my ears
    Of all the lost adventurers my peers,—
How such a one was strong, and such was bold,
And such was fortunate, yet each of old
    Lost, lost! one moment knelled the woe of years.

There they stood, ranged along the hill-sides, met
    To view the last of me, a living frame
    For one more picture! in a sheet of flame
I saw them and I knew them all. And yet
Dauntless the slug-horn to my lips I set,
    And blew. *'Childe Roland to the Dark Tower came.'*

## Epilogue from Ferishtah's Fancies

T̲he third, fourth, fifth and sixth stanzas of this poem, quoted out of context, are often used to suggest that striving for 'perfection, nothing less' gives, in its own way, immortality to those who strive. But within the structure of the poems as a whole these stanzas reveal that note of ambiguity and questioning which is present in so many of Browning's apparently optimistic statements.

Oh, Love—no, Love! All the noise below, Love,
   Groanings all and moanings—none of Life I lose!
All of Life's a cry just of weariness and woe, Love—
   'Hear at least, thou happy one!' How can I, Love, but choose?

Only, when I do hear, sudden circle round me
   —Much as when the moon's might frees a space from cloud—
Iridescent splendours: gloom—would else confound me—
   Barriered off and banished far—bright-edged the blackest shroud!

Thronging through the cloud-rift, whose are they, the faces
   Faint revealed yet sure divined, the famous ones of old?
'What'—they smile—'our names, our deeds so soon erases
   Time upon his tablet where Life's glory lies enrolled?

'Was it for mere fool's-play, make-believe and mumming.
  So we battled it like men, not boylike sulked or whined?
Each of us heard clang God's "Come!" and each was coming
  Soldiers all, to forward-face, not sneaks to lag behind!

'How of the field's fortune! That concerned our Leader!
  Led, we struck our stroke nor cared for doings left and right
Each as on his sole head, failer or succeeder,
  Lay the blame or lit the praise: no care for cowards: fight!

Then the cloud-rift broadens, spanning earth that's under
  Wide our world displays its worth, man's strife and strife's success:
All the good and beauty, wonder crowning wonder,
  Till my heart and soul applaud perfection, nothing less.

Only, at heart's utmost joy and triumph, terror
  Sudden turns the blood to ice: a chill wind disencharms
All the late enchantment! What if all be error—
  If the halo irised round my head were, Love, thine arms?

Since Browning was sure of being answerable to God for the whole of life, there runs through his poetry a sense of the judgement to which, in the end, we must answer for our conduct of our God-given life. The poem 'Easter Day', with which we began, faces this issue squarely. Its closing lines reflect Browning's overwhelming sense of the love of God, and the hopeful prayerfulness with which he therefore faces God's judgement. Yet he is still questioning...'who can say?' It is therefore fitting to close this selection with a further extract from 'Easter Day', in which Browning wrestles with that question.

F·R·O·M
## Easter Day

The central character has belatedly come to the conclusion, faced with choice about the basis of life, that 'love is best', and the towering and transcendent figure of the Christ, to whose hem he is clinging, replies:

'Is this thy final choice?
Love is the best? 'Tis somewhat late!
And all thou dost enumerate
Of power and beauty in the world,
The mightiness of love was curled
Inextricably round about.
Love lay within it and without,
To clasp thee,—but in vain! Thy soul
Still shrunk from Him who made the whole,
Still set deliberate aside
His love!—Now take love! Well betide
Thy tardy conscience! Haste to take
The show of love for the name's sake,
Remembering every moment Who,
Beside creating thee unto
These ends, and these for thee, was said
To undergo death in thy stead

In flesh like thine: so ran the tale.
What doubt in thee could countervail
Belief in it? Upon the ground
"That in the story had been found
Too much love! How could God love so?"
He who in all his works below
Adapted to the needs of man,
Made love the basis of the plan,—
Did love, as was demonstrated:
While man, who was so fit instead
To hate, as every day gave proof,—
Man thought man, for his kind's behoof,
Both could and did invent that scheme
Of perfect love: 'twould well beseem
Cain's nature thou wast wont to praise,
Not tally with God's usual ways!'

And I cowered deprecatingly—
'Thou Love of God! Or let me die,
Or grant what shall seem heaven almost!
Let me not know that all is lost,
Though lost it be—leave me not tied
To this despair, this corpse-like bride!
Let that old life seem mine—no more—
With limitation as before,
With darkness, hunger, toil, distress:
Be all the earth a wilderness!
Only let me go on, go on,
Still hoping ever and anon
To reach one eve the Better Land!'

Then did the form expand, expand—
I knew Him through the dread disguise
As the whole God within His eyes
Embraced me...

Thank God, no paradise stands barred
To entry, and I find it hard
To be a Christian, as I said!
Still every now and then my head
Raised glad, sinks mournful—all grows drear

Spite of the sunshine, while I fear
And think, 'How dreadful to be grudged
No ease henceforth, as one that's judged,
Condemned to earth for ever, shut
From heaven!'
    But Easter-Day breaks! But
Christ rises! Mercy every way
Is infinite,—and who can say?

# NOTES AND SOURCES

*Pages 9 and 43*
'Easter Day', ll. 1,2, 9-12, 29-37
First published in *Christmas-Eve and Easter-Day*, 1850. The context of the volume is the death of Browning's mother in 1849, the birth of his son in the same year, and the challenge of his wife, Elizabeth Barrett Browning (herself a woman of strong Christian faith), that he should speak directly about his own Christian beliefs and difficulties.

*Page 10*
'Bishop Blougram's Apology', ll. 150-197
First published in *Men and Women*, 1855, and underwent some revision in later editions. Browning acknowledged that Cardinal Wiseman, the controversial Roman Catholic Archbishop of Westminster from 1850, served as his model for Blougram. The word 'Apology' is ambiguous. It hints both at expressing regret for a fault, and at justifying a position held, or an act perpetrated: *apologia*.

*Page 12*
'A Death in the Desert', ll. 133-162, 176-182, 188-197, 235-238 and 474-476.
First published in *Dramatis Personae*, 1864, this poem is clearly written in the context of the 'Higher Criticism' debate, and in particular is responding to work by Strauss, Renan and Feuerbach. Browning was deeply influenced by the Gospel of St John, whose doctrine of God as Love was at the heart of his own faith. He appears to view the writer of Revelation as the same John to whom the Gospel and Letters are attributed.

*Page 14*
'Christmas-Eve', ll. 261-284, 1170-1187, 1203-1210
See notes on 'Easter Day', above. The letter quoted was written by Browning to Elizabeth Barrett on 17 August 1846. (See *Letters II*, 436.)

*Page 17*
'Fra Lippo Lippi', ll. 217-220, 265-269, 280-315
First published in *Men and Women*, 1855, the views put into Fra Lippo Lippi's mouth are generally held to be those of Browning himself, and repeat in verse form much of what he had said, in his essay on Shelley, of the task of the artist.

*Page 19*
'Pippa Passes', Part I, ll. 221-236
First published in 1841, in the series *Bells and Pomegranates*, conceived as a 'Drama', Browning said it was of 'someone walking alone through life; one apparently too obscure to leave a trace of his or her passage, yet exercising a lasting though unconscious influence at every step of it' (Mrs Orr, *Handbook*, 55).

*Page 20*
'Saul', ll. 238-312
First published in full in *Men and Women* in 1855, though the earlier parts of it appeared in *Dramatic Romances and Lyrics* in 1845, and again in 1849. Its religious vision has much in common with 'An Epistle...of Karshish', (see below) and it is generally thought both poems were completed by 1853. It was one of Browning's own favourites, and chosen by him as one of his four most representative poems.

*Page 23*
'Abt Vogler', ll. 65-88
First published in *Dramatis Personae*, 1864. Abbe Vogler, a German musician, had taught John Relfe, Browning's own music teacher. This was another of the four poems Browning chose as most representative of his work.

*Page 25*
'Rabbi ben Ezra', ll. 1-6, 85-108, 145-162, 181-190
First published in *Dramatis Personae*, 1864. Abraham ben Ezra (1092-1167), a Spanish Jew, is used by Browning as his own spokesman. Amongst his most popular poems, it was asked for by Thomas Hardy on his death-bed. (Ironically, in view of Hardy's earlier dismissal of Browning's 'smug Christian optimism' as 'worthy of a dissenting grocer' and out of place 'inside a man who was so vast a seer and father when on neutral ground'.)

*Page 27*
'Christmas Eve', ll. 583-593
See note above. Elizabeth Barrett's letter was written to Browning on 15 August 1846. (See *Letters II*, 429-430.)

*Page 28*
'An Epistle...of Karshish', ll. 97-112, 178-212, 243-276, 304-312.
First published in *Men and Women*, 1855, this poem, particularly the last section, should be read in conjunction with 'Saul' (see above). It is based on the Gospel of St John, chapter 11, verses 1-44.

*Page 31*
'Prospice'
Probably written soon after Elizabeth Barrett Browning's death in 1861, it was first published in the *Atlantic Monthly XVIII* and then in *Dramatis Personae*, 1864.

*Page 32*
'Pauline', ll. 821-830
First published anonymously in 1833, and sold not a single copy! Strongly autobiographical, its chief quality is its open exposition of Shelley's influence on Browning.

*Page 33*
'Life in a Love'
One of two companion pieces (with 'Love in a Life') first published in *Men and Women*, 1855. Browning wrote to Elizabeth Barrett on 5 April 1846, 'In this House of Life—where I go, you go—where I ascend you run before—where I descend, it is after you.'

*Page 34*
'De Gustibus—'
The title is based on the Latin proverb, 'De Gustibus non est disputandum': 'About tastes there is no arguing'. First published in *Men and Women*, 1855.

*Page 36*
'Home-thoughts, from the Sea'
Originally a third section in a poem which began with the lines now collected as a separate poem, 'Home-thoughts from Abroad', and published in *Dramatic Romances and Lyrics*, 1845. It was separated in 1849 and given its present title; and included in 'Lyrics' in 1863.

*Page 37*
'Epilogue'
First published in *Asolando*, December, 1889 and post-dated 1890. Browning died in the evening of its publication. He had read it in proof to his daughter-in-law and sister, just before his last illness, and said of these stanzas, 'It sounds like bragging to say this, and as if I ought to cancel it; but it's the simple truth; and as it's true, it shall stand.'

*Page 38*
'Childe Roland to the Dark Tower came', ll. 37-60, 73-78, 109-126, 157-204
Browning said of this poem that it came upon him 'as a kind of dream' that had to be written, and 'very fond' of it as he was, it was 'only a fantasy' with 'no allegorical intention'. But when asked whether 'he that endureth to the end shall be saved' summed it up, he replied, 'Just about that'. It was first published in *Men and Women*, 1855.

*Page 41*
'Epilogue' from *Ferishtah's Fancies*
*Ferishtah's Fancies* was published in 1884. (The Epilogue was dated December, 1883, and may not originally have been intended for this volume.) 'Ferishtah' means 'Fairy'.

*Page 43*
'Easter Day', ll. 958-1007, 1029-1040
See first note above.